A strip of metal, bent into a loop, offering resistance only until it is soldered. In this, the moment of most extreme resistance, it attains its most relaxed, most natural form, and in the greatest tension, its greatest serenity. And only then.

Ilse Aichinger

For Antunin

PETER ZUMTHOR

1985–1989

Buildings and Projects

Volume 1

Edited by Thomas Durisch

Scheidegger & Spiess

What I Do

The five volumes in this monograph present a record of my work as an architect since 1985. However, prior to that, I had already worked in the field of historical preservation, renovated chapels, and remodeled old buildings. My first new building was erected in Haldenstein in 1976. These early projects are not included here. They come from a time in which I started out working in a more playful and carefree vein, and later increasingly under the influence of role models. From the late 1970s to the mid-1980s, where the present documentation sets in, young architects in German-speaking Switzerland were caught up in something that affected me as well and to which I gradually felt I belonged. I met architects not only at home but in Vorarlberg, Vienna, and Ticino. We talked about the visual quality of architecture, its sensuality, its physicality, its ability to create atmosphere. Aldo Rossi, who was teaching in Zurich at the time, opened my eyes to the history of architecture and the architecture of my biographical memory. The journal *archithese* founded by Stanislaus von Moos addressed such issues as monotony, realism in architecture, and *Learning from Las Vegas*.

It was an extraordinarily exciting time for me. I felt liberated and started designing new buildings in my own way. I think I had acquired enough background knowledge by then to jettison the ideological ballast that had accumulated in the politically oriented years after 1968, freighting notions of design, both mine and those of others. I started to trust in my own ideas again. I remember the wonderful sense of freedom and certainty, a kind of blissful tension. It was a time of awakening. There was something in the air. My personal search had begun.

I had felt that way once before, as a very young cabinetmaker with a diploma in my pocket at what is now known as the University of Art and Design in Basel. We lovingly called it "our trade school" when—having already drawn and built furniture of my own—I started designing furniture and interiors under the guidance of the instructors. That, too, was a time of great freedom for me, despite the restrictions of Classical Modernism, which, as everyone knows, did not have a particularly good relationship to the history of architecture. But that didn't bother me because it was closely linked to the wonderful feeling that good design always has to chart new territory. So by the nineteen-eighties, I had come full circle.

And now, many years later, they are all spread out before me, the buildings and projects that have emerged since 1985 out of that initial momentum. I like looking at all the designs again and can still feel the enthusiasm, the hard work, and the passion that went into them. The people and the dreams related to the projects come to mind again, too.

We would love to build that! How often did we say that to ourselves when we felt we had come up with the right form for the task and the site. Great and sobering was the disappointment when, as so often, it did not come about. When I look at the buildings that were not executed, I still have the feeling that they were good buildings and would have been an enrichment for the place and perhaps the client as well. In the case of other designs that never materialized, I think that fate might have been merciful by sparing us something from which we were bound and determined not to be spared. For instance, the building for the Topography of Terror in Berlin met with so many difficulties that, as the years passed, practically no one wanted it anymore, neither client nor users, while the few who still did want it would have preferred to build something much simpler. If we had had to build this extremely demanding building after all, would we have managed to cope? Wouldn't the project have been too difficult without the support of a client who believed in the design? At the same time we were mastering substantial challenges in Cologne. We were at the most intense stage of planning and would soon break ground for the Kolumba Art Museum. There we had a client who appreciated our design and worked on it with us. We had the same stroke of luck with the Therme Vals building committee and with representatives of the Swiss Confederation, with whom we were able to execute the Swiss Pavilion at the Expo 2000 in Hanover. In retrospect, I realize that we were basically always lucky when we were able to build. For that I am grateful.

In the course of planning the Art Museum in Bregenz, the project ran into stormy political waters and we are indebted to a small group of locals, the curators of the museum, and a few construction experts who helped us stay on course. After the museum opened, the problems that had beset the project were soon forgotten and many people were more than willing to take the credit. I cannot deny a certain bitterness in that regard because the prolonged and trying experience in Bregenz, when there were few people left who believed in our design and our ability to construct and build the museum, took its toll on my family. Later, my wife told me that I was so caught up in the situation that I barely took note of her and the children. Now the bitterness has all but vanished and I can appreciate the great challenges in planning and building, faced not only by us architects and contractors, but also by the clients and users of our buildings—those who had to endure a method that precludes easy compromise. Looking back, I think it is a good thing that difficulties overcome are soon forgotten. Many people are pleased with the outcome, including the former worrywarts and skeptics. The completed building is your best argument, a client once said to me.

On revisiting other designs in these volumes, I still think: what a pity they weren't built! The little hotel tower in the Engadine, the art gallery in Berlin, the winery in Duero Valle in Spain, the Herz Jesu Church in Munich, the Laban Centre in London, the summer restaurant on an island in Lake Zurich, the hotel in the Atacama Desert in Chile. The list is long. I shall cut it short and abandon the path of old disappointments in order to speak instead of a wonderful and comforting discovery. When I look at my unbuilt designs, I realize that once an architectural thought has been conceived and converted into a stringent and coherent form, it does not simply vanish out of sight and out of mind; it reappears in other designs. Certain fundamental ideas keep coming back in new contexts and they seem to acquire ever more depth the more often they rise to the surface.

However, even though single ideas recur, the buildings and projects documented in these volumes are very different from each other. What they share is my wish and belief that, if I devote myself carefully enough to the study of a building's purpose and the place it will occupy and to their reciprocal relationship, an architectural form will emerge almost by itself, as it were. Purpose and place and everything I know generate a tension that in turn generates the design.

I like designing buildings in response to a place. Places fascinate me. I love devising spaces whose form and atmosphere perfectly match their use. Long before I became an architect, I was invariably impressed by atmospherically dense spaces.

What is required? What should be built? Where should it be situated? What would work well in the process of use? What would look good and right on the site? I ask myself these questions and look for the coherence that makes for a beautiful and self-evident correlation of form and content. Ideally, the building will match its use, just as a glove fits the hand. Its beauty will be a pleasure for the people who use it and it will have a presence that enriches its surroundings.

To me, finding the right form for a building means thinking over and over about what it is used for and how. As work on the design progresses, our ideas on what the building has to offer and how it is to be used become more and more precise. In cooperation with our clients, we question and examine the specifications of the initial program: we confirm, reject, revise, and add to them. Thanks to this procedure, when we have finished our work on the design, we know more than we did at the beginning. For instance, we used the original spatial program of Therme Vals as the point of departure for thinking about what a thermal bath might be like in the mountains. The answers that we subsequently found and built actually yielded more and different things than what was required or the client even realized in the original specifications.

As an architect I am an author. I do not want to find forms for content that leaves me no room to do any thinking on my own and that I cannot influence in any way. I want to contribute to working out and formulating the content of my buildings. Every architectural design must be able to question abstract specifications, because one can determine whether abstract preliminary thoughts will work only when they acquire concrete, physical shape. I have to work that way. I design my buildings from the inside out and from the outside in and then once again from inside out until everything is right.

Atelier Zumthor, Haldenstein, Graubünden
1985–1986

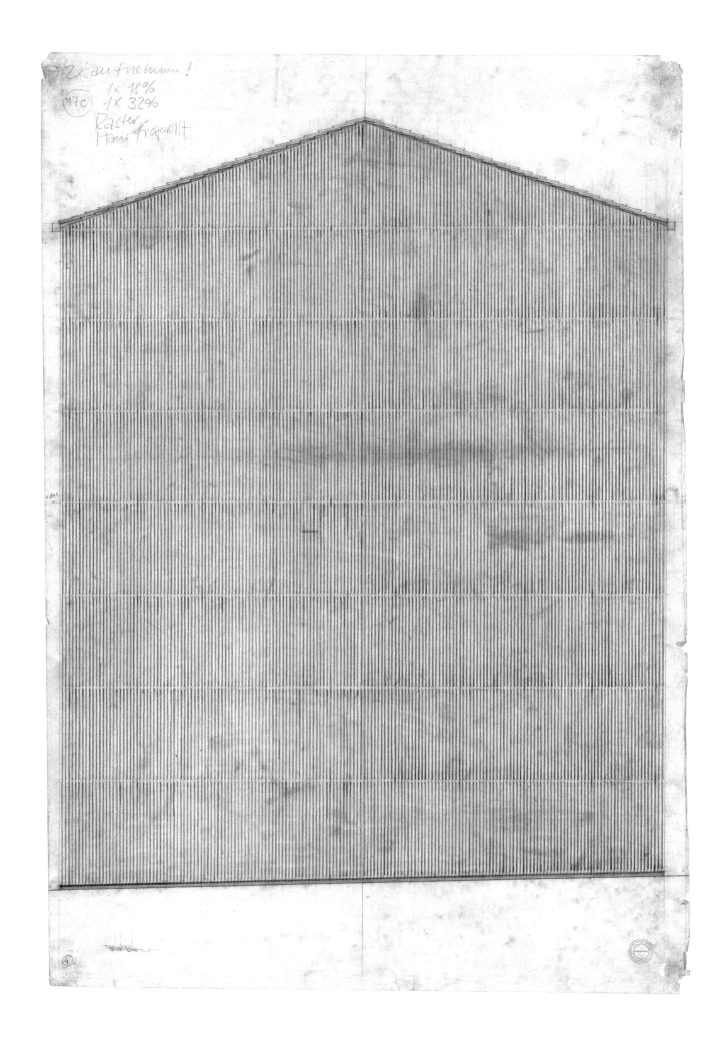

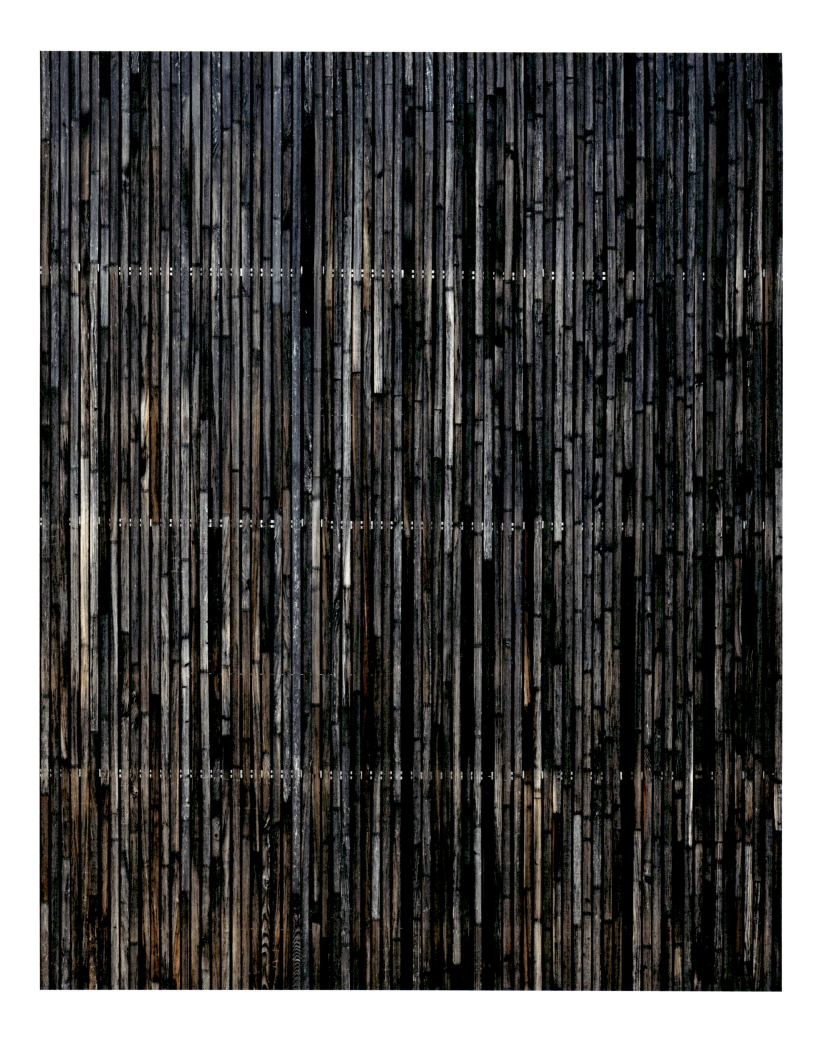

After we had been living for over ten years in our renovated farmhouse in the Suesswinkelgasse, I finally overcame the objections of the town and cantonal authorities, who (for aesthetic reasons) had refused to grant building permits for my first new construction projects back in the early nineteen-eighties, and built a studio for myself and my family. We conceived it as a garden house for all of us. It contained a garden room on the ground floor and a drawing studio on the second floor. Lying in front of the house is a tiny park with square plots of land, a strip of water, and Japanese cherry trees.

The conventional timber-frame construction was given a delicate, cabinetry-like façade of larch-wood, which binds the whole structure together and emphasizes its volume. It was important to set an example here of clarity and repose, as against the heavy, rustic Alpine style widely used back then in new constructions. The works of Donald Judd and other artists of the time, reductions to basic volumetric shapes, had impressed me. I was looking for a simple construction for my studio that would fit in with the organic surroundings of a farming community in a non-spectacular fashion. And with a conscious selection of materials I wanted to create a sensual expression of a building which just grew naturally out of itself: larch-wood, pieces of flat iron, hardware fittings arranged ornamentally, hiding the nails that hold the curtain of sticks to the façade, oak for the pergola, awnings of bright fabric, natural red tiles on the roof.

In the interior of the building the artist Matias Spescha created a breathing surface of calico mesh: its texture is reminiscent of the painting style of Mark Rothko. A pergola shades the south window—a layer of light and shade between inside and outside, in which grapevines grow before the awnings which flap in the wind. The footprint of the building is in principle one single large interior, divided by a long wall. The structure is open in front of this wall. The windows look out on a small rectangular flower garden set into the irregular growth of the surroundings to the south.

I like working near a long wall that keeps the area behind me clear and protected. I always find it a luxury and a privilege just to sit alone in the room by the long wall, working, looking at the cherry trees, seeing the children at play. The spot gives me a feeling of ease, of strength. Looking back, I think it was good for my work as an architect to have this spot—a place of my own for living and working, with my family nearby. The studio was the germ cell of a small campus for architecture in this farming village. It was the first in the process of weaving several new buildings into the structure of the village street.

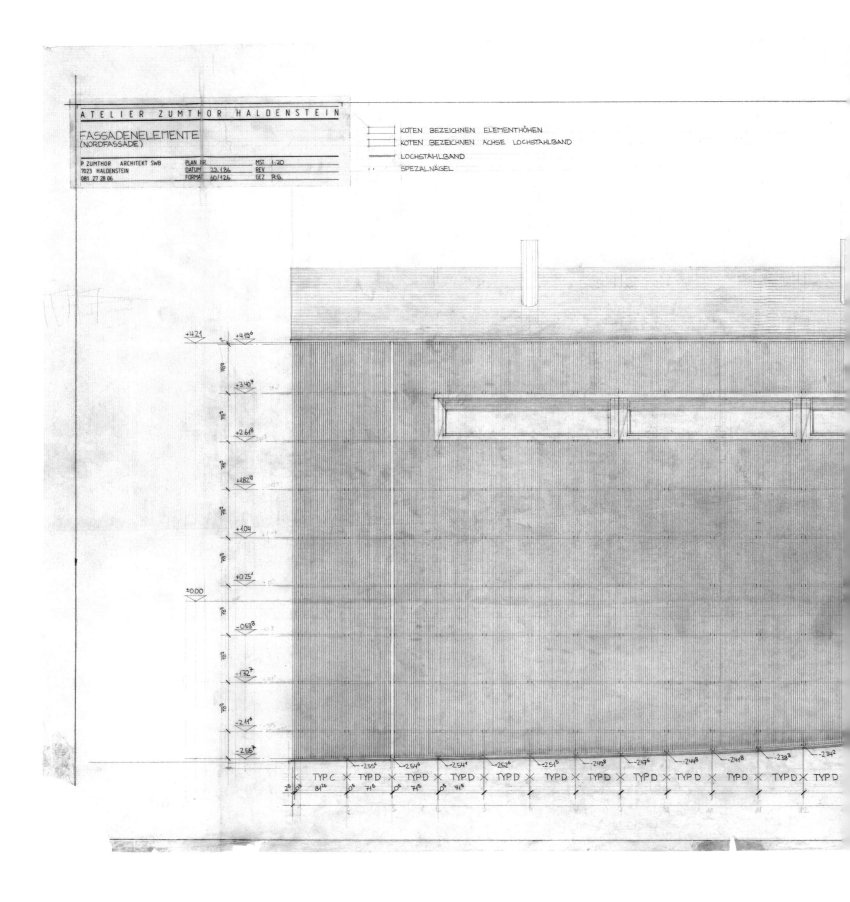

ATELIER ZUMTHOR HALDENSTEIN

FASSADENELEMENTE
(NORDFASSADE)

P. ZUMTHOR ARCHITEKT SWB	PLAN NR 23.1.86	MST 1:20
7023 HALDENSTEIN	DATUM 23.1.86	REV
081 27 28 06	FORMAT 60/426	GEZ R.S.

KOTEN BEZEICHNEN ELEMENTHÖHEN

KOTEN BEZEICHNEN ACHSE LOCHSTAHLBAND

LOCHSTAHLBAND

SPEZIALNÄGEL

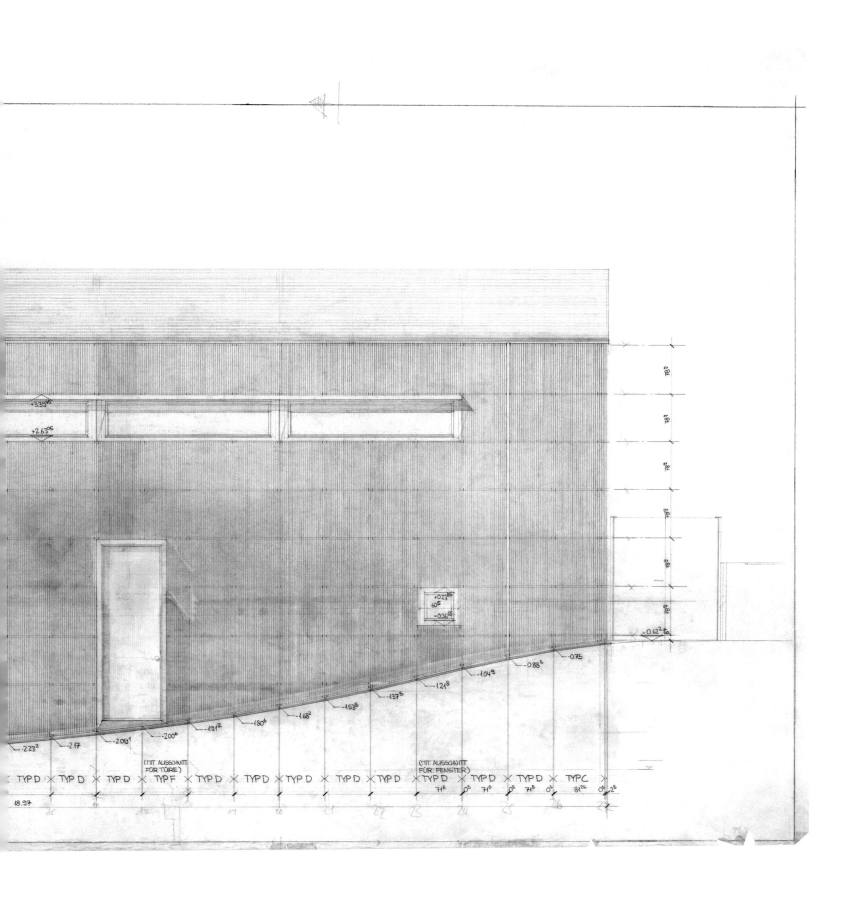

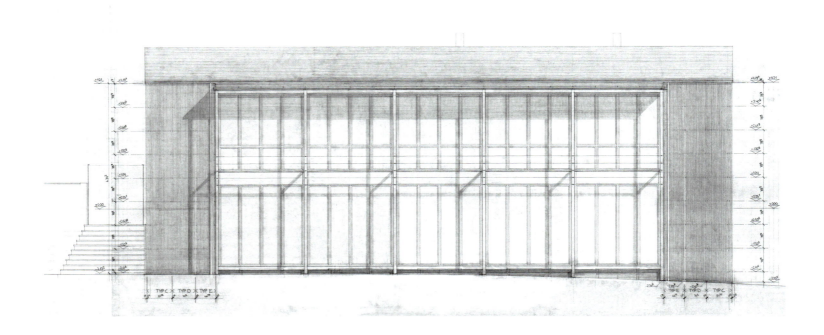

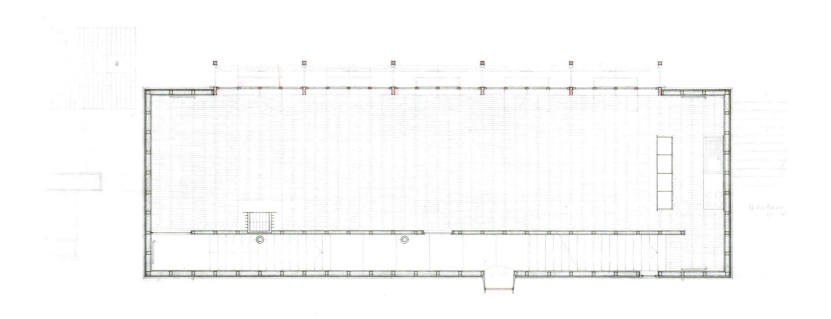

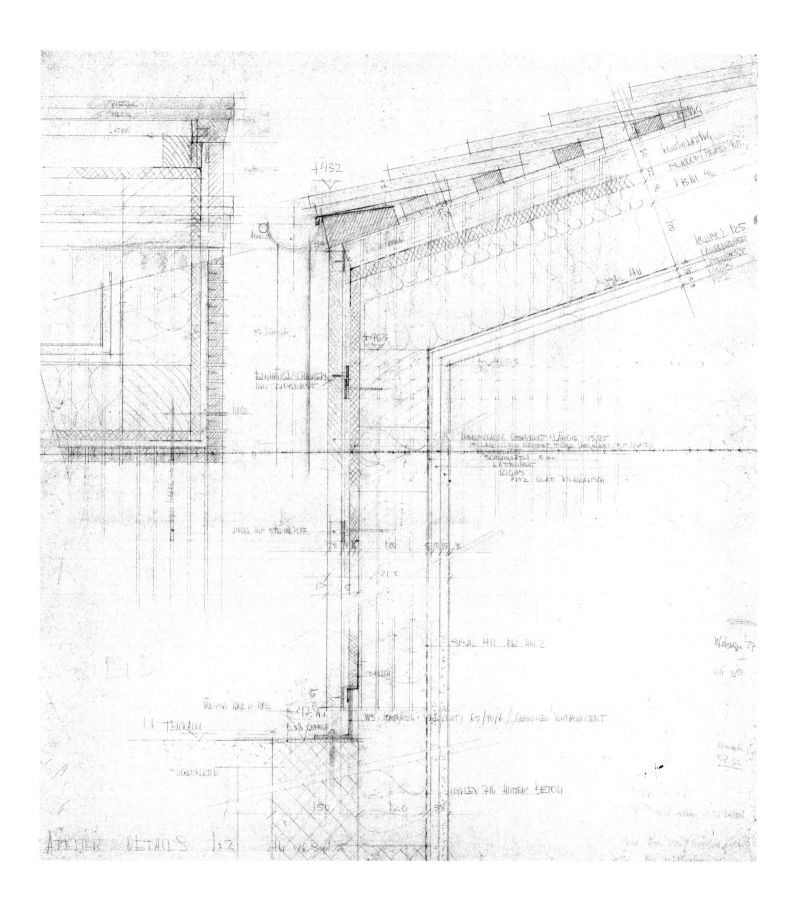

ATELIER DETAILS 1:2

Shelter for Roman Archaeological Ruins, Chur, Graubünden
1985–1986

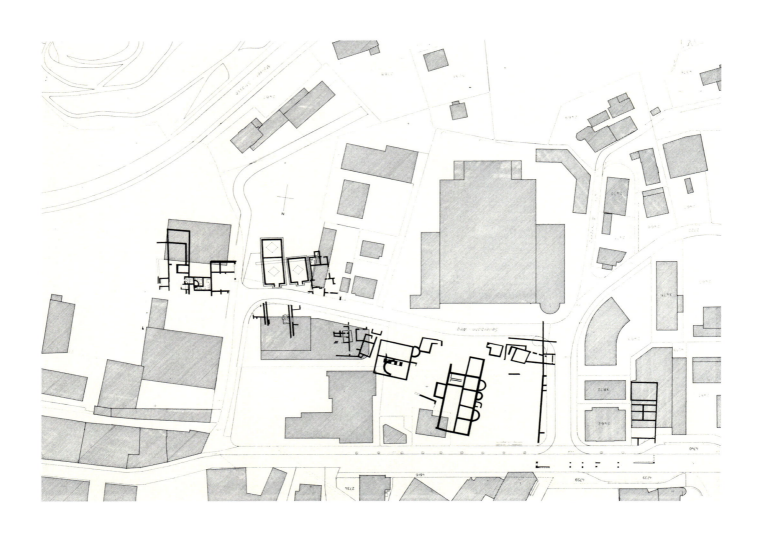

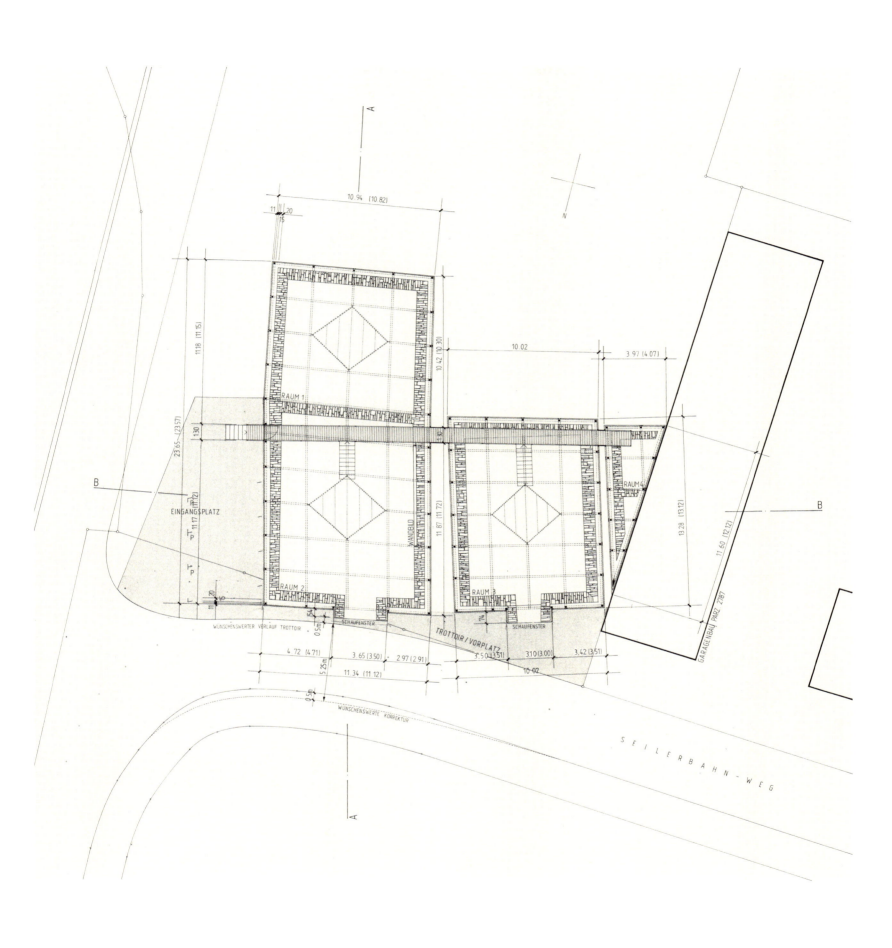

Not much is known about Chur in Roman times, and there is hardly anything left to see. This explains the desire to leave exposed the relatively modest masonry remains of two Roman commercial structures and make them accessible to the public.

Our project is a small museum. To visit the building, which has no staff, you must arrange to pick up the key in town against a deposit. However, two display windows above the original Roman entry doors also afford a view into the building from outside.

The wooden protective sheathing exactly follows the excavated foundation walls of the Roman structure, making it easier to envision the size and shape of the lost buildings. It creates a volumetric presence in the urban space, and in the interior one can sense the long-lost rooms. For the sake of conservation, the protective shells are permeable to air. At night, passersby can switch lights on inside, making the shells look like lanterns in the cityscape.

On entering the structures, you become aware of the noises of the city penetrating the open louvered structure, while the view to the outside is blocked off except for the two display windows over the Roman doors, which now seem like windows on the city. When you stand between the almost 1800-year-old walls, indirect daylight illuminates their wooden "fins," also revealing the Roman remains of a charred wooden floor, found objects, and a remounted fragment of a wall painting depicting Mercury, the god of commerce and thieves: you are steeped in history and you hear the city of the present.

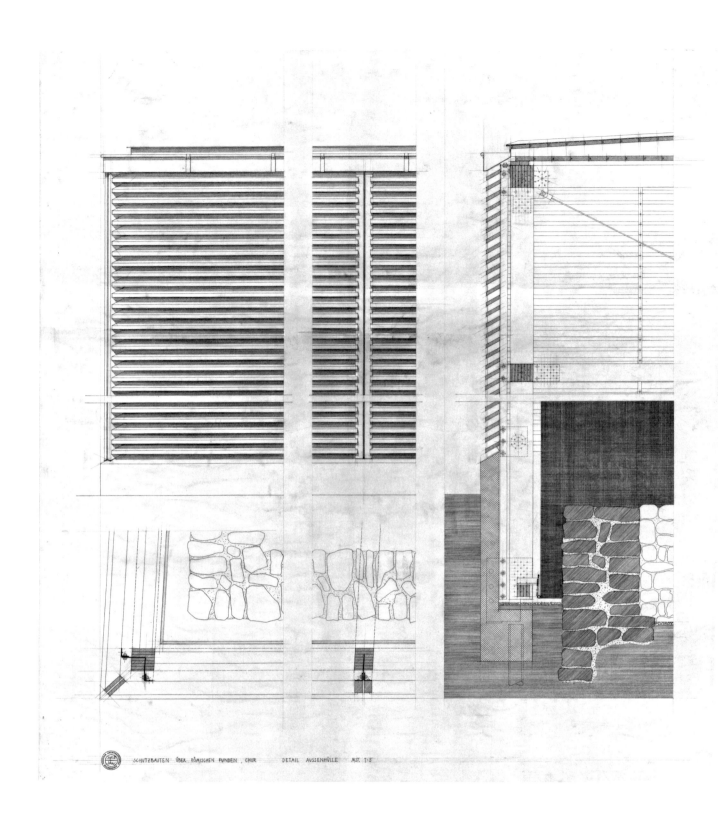

SCHUTZBAUTEN ÜBER RÖMISCHEN FUNDEN, CHUR   DETAIL AUSSENHÜLLE   MST. 1:5

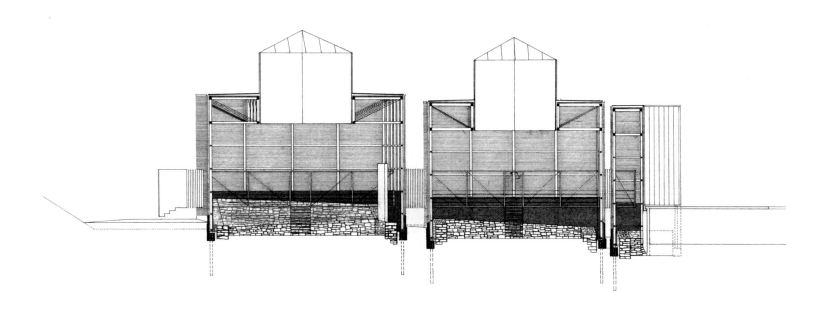

Caplutta Sogn Benedetg, Sumvitg, Graubünden
1985–1988

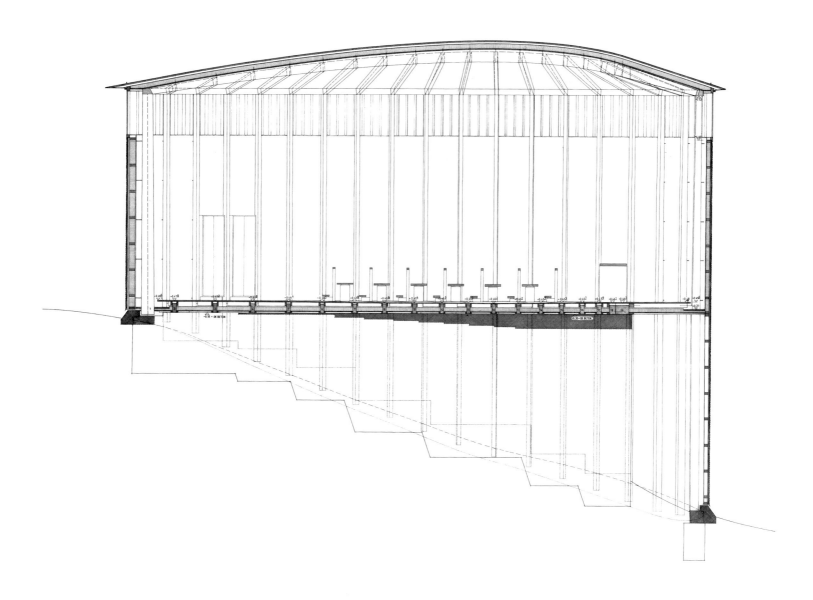

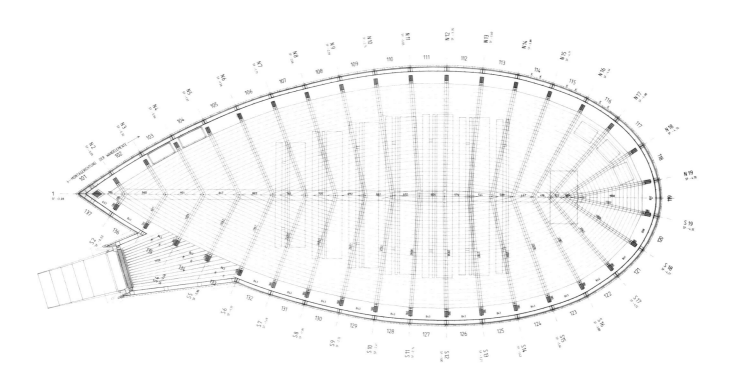

N

0   1   2

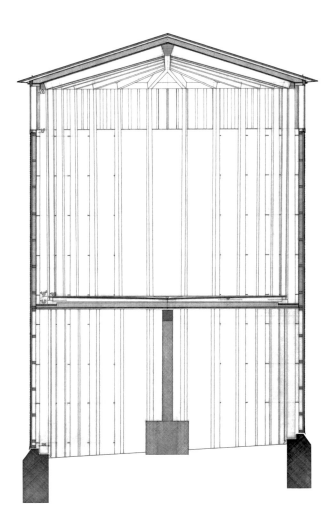

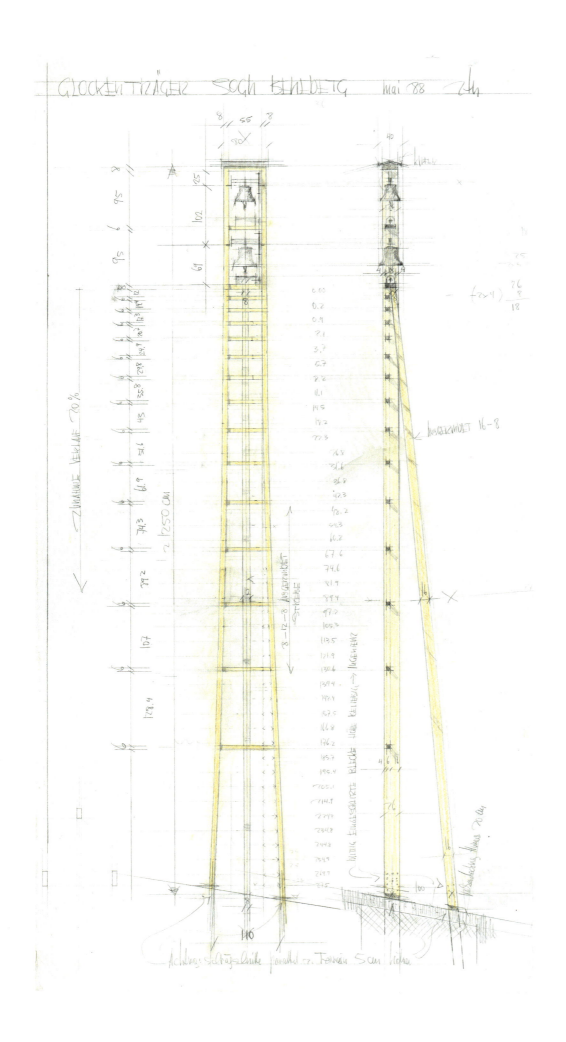

In 1984 an avalanche destroyed the Baroque chapel at the entrance to Sogn Benedetg, because a parking lot which had been filled in forced a huge slab of snow like a ramp up to the chapel. The new site on an old mountain trail above the hamlet is protected from avalanches by the forest above.

The wooden chapel, mantled with larch-wood shingles, was inaugurated in 1988. Three years earlier the community had granted us the building permit with the comment "senza perschuasiun," without conviction. But the prelates of the Disentis Monastery and the village pastor Martin Bearth wanted to build something new and contemporary for future generations. A leaf, an eye, a fish, a boat, a wedge to divert avalanches—it pleases me to hear these interpretations of the form of this little church, but the actual story of how it came to be is different. The specifications of the competition enabled us to conceive of the chapel as a single space. The idea that its exterior form would be defined by a single interior space fascinated me. This is the notion of a simple vessel. I wanted to find a soft, maternal form for my vessel. Even as a young boy I had had my problems with the authoritarian, indoctrinating church; so a predominating, geometrical form such as a square, a circle, or a rectangle was out of the question for me. Our engineer Jürg Conzett took my original freehand sketch and defined it geometrically as half of a lemniscate.

The Surselva region of Graubünden, where the chapel is located, is full of Baroque chapels wonderfully placed in the landscape—white plasterwork gems from the Counterreformation, standing alone in the meadow. Our Sogn Benedetg also stands alone in the meadow. The wooden pasture fencing, taken down every winter by the farmers before the first snow, directly abuts the chapel. But Sogn Benedetg, unlike the white Baroque chapels of the region, is made of wood. Its structure ages beautifully with the weather; it has become dark and darker on the south side, and silvery on the north.

Perhaps the chapel is a little wooden boat after all, built for an uncertain journey by local people born into the heritage of building with wood.

Spittelhof Housing Complex, Biel-Benken near Basel
1987–1996

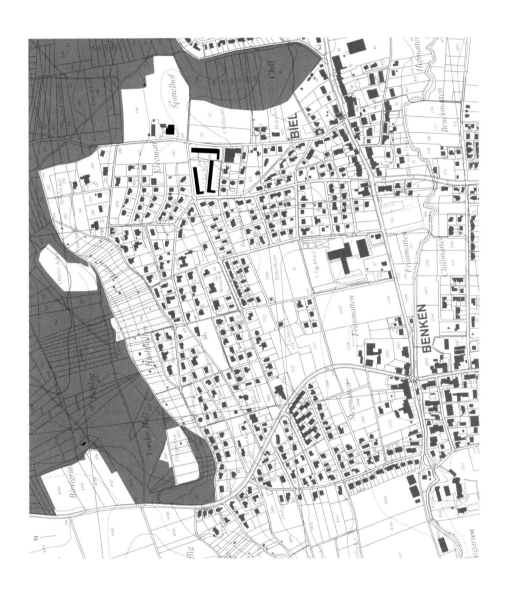

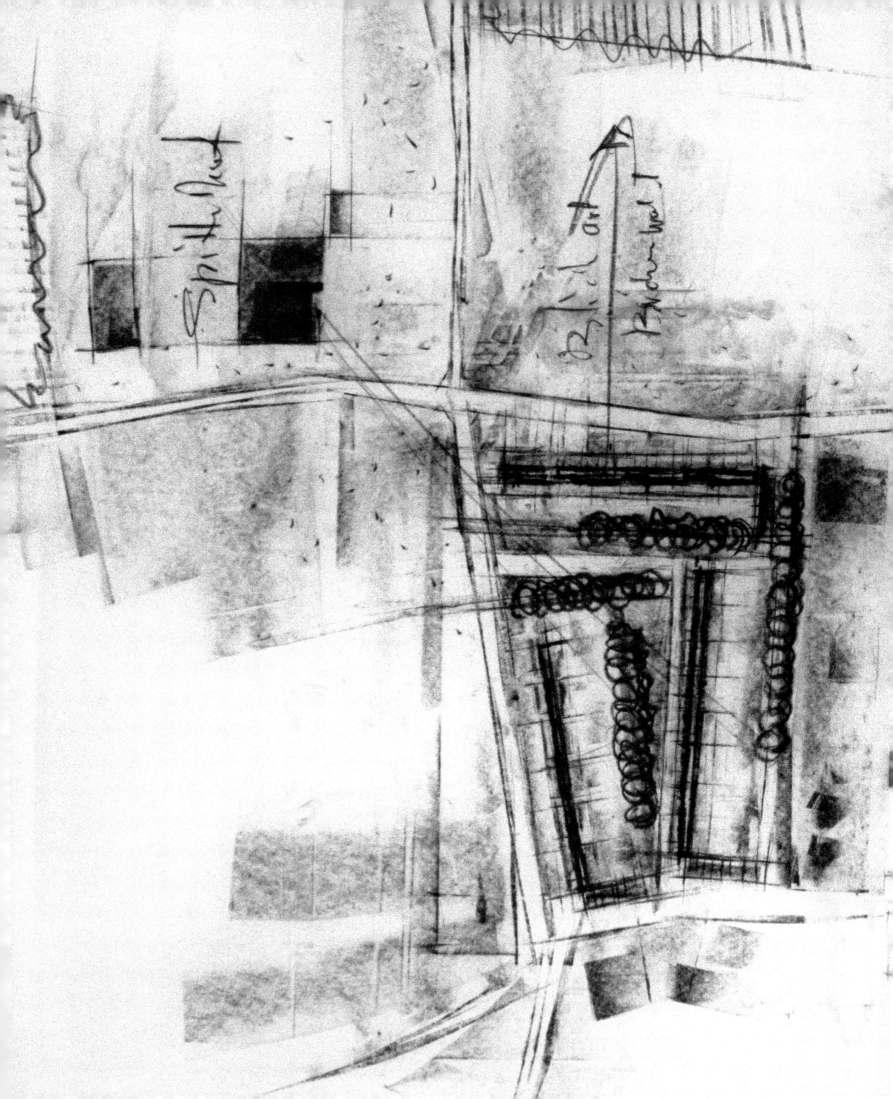

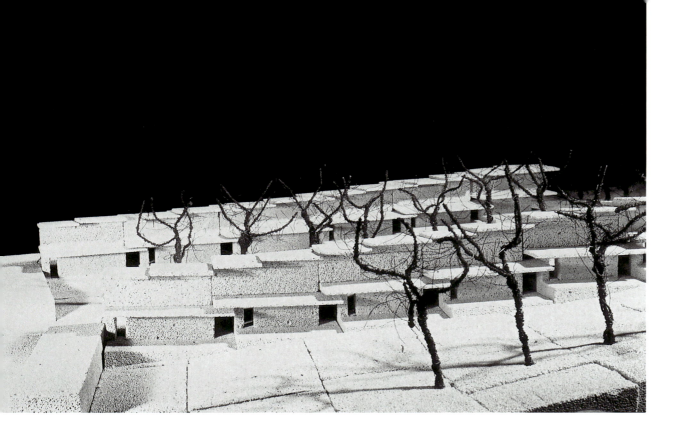

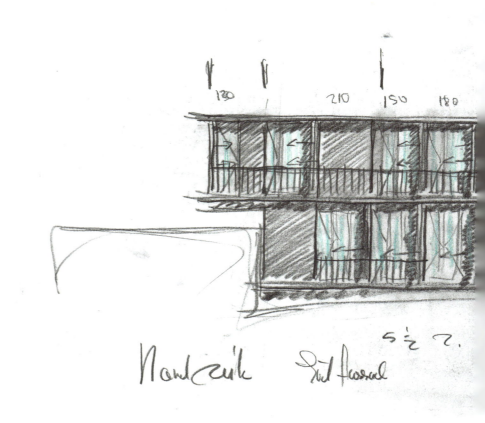

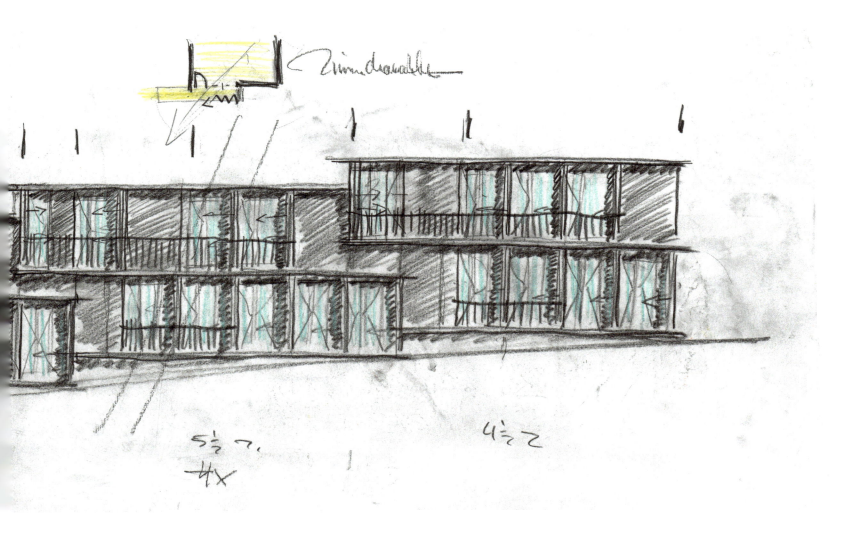

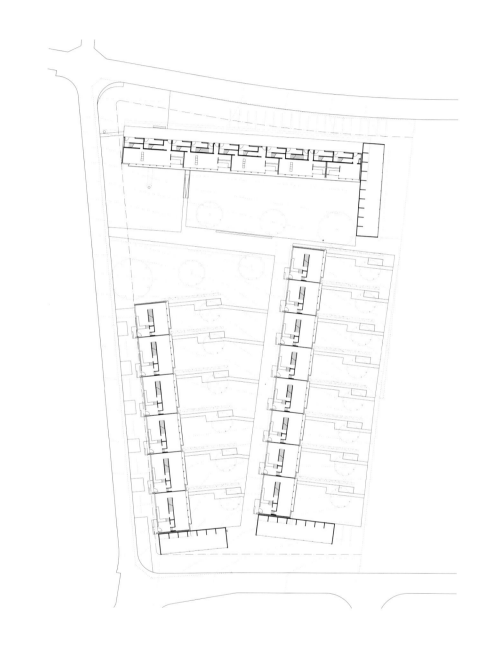

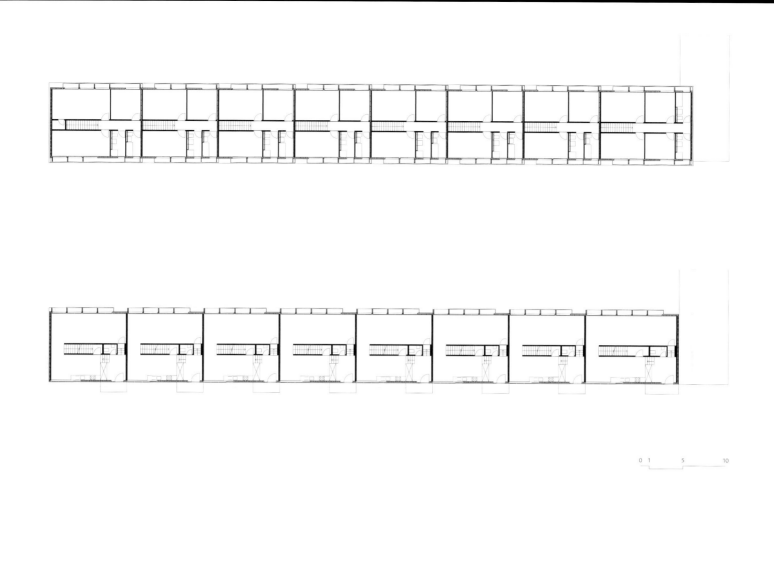

0 1   5   10

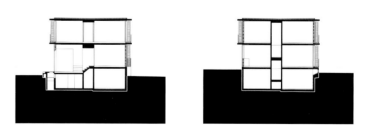

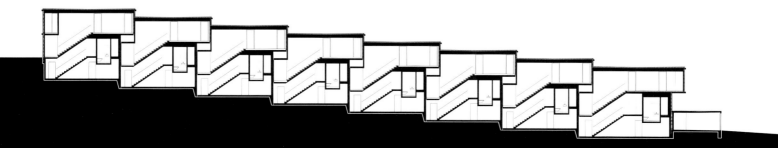

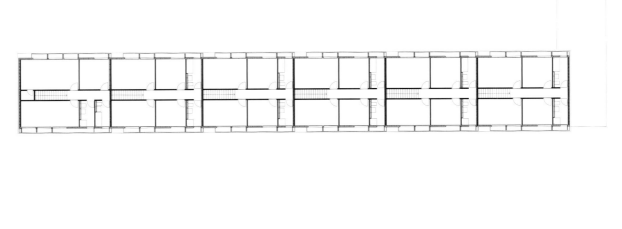

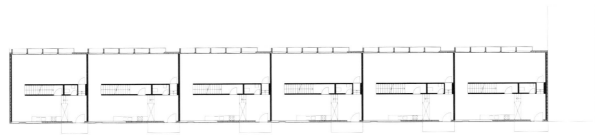

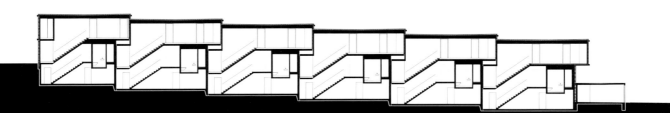

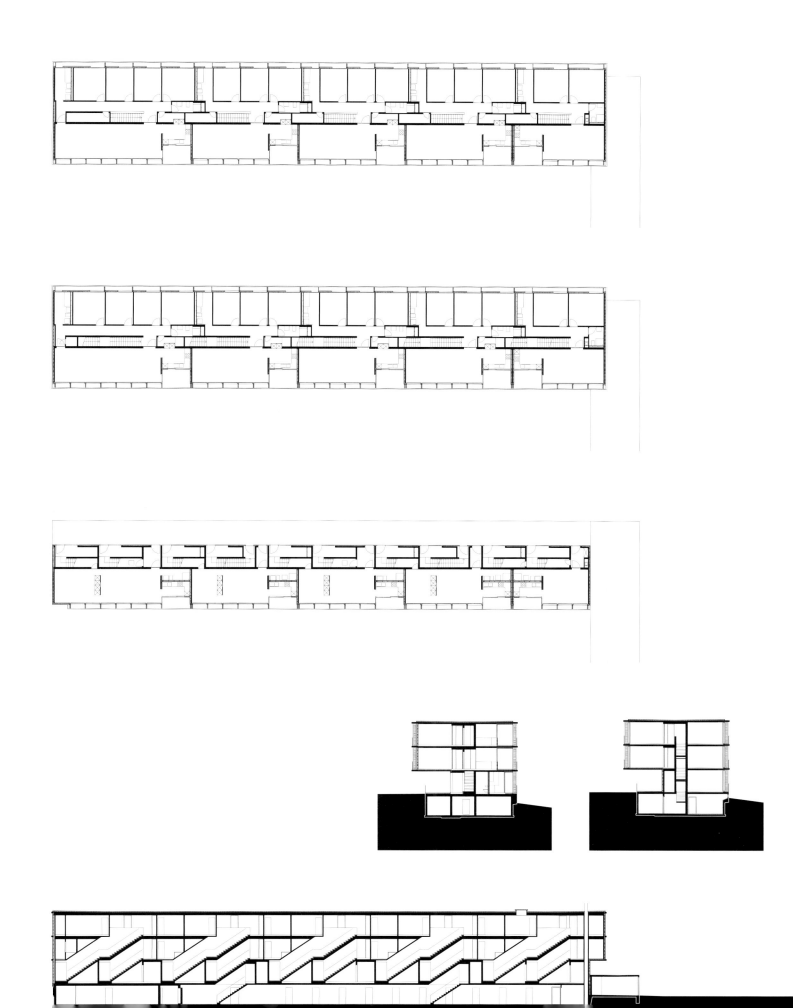

Spittelhof, a historic farmstead in Biel-Benken, is a good residential site. The nearby city of Basel lies behind it, and in front it looks out at the woods and fields of the beautiful Sundgau countryside in neighboring Alsace. There is hardly any traffic noise. In this landscape, where well-off people favor fenced-in single family houses and villas, building a housing complex is something special. The community of Biel-Benken, the owner of the land, wanted to make a statement about the economical use of land.

I love the idea of architects defining the overall form and shape of a housing colony. In this way you can achieve a goodly measure of openness and scale, and create good addresses where people will want to live. The large Berlin and Frankfurt housing complexes of the early twentieth century by Bruno Taut, Hugo Häring, Hans Scharoun, or Ernst May have always impressed me. They offer not just good living space, but also nice gradations of public and private outdoor spaces, and I believe I sense the intention of planners and architects of that period: not to overwhelm or anonymize the future residents of their complexes with excessive architectural scale and mass.

That is a challenging context for a small housing complex out in the country with barely thirty living units. Nonetheless, we did try a few things: the three long oblong structures together form a large courtyard and gardens that open onto the historic Spittelhof, and semi-public walkways link up with the village's network of paths.

The gently inclined rows of houses with their south-facing gardens trace the topographical sweep of the site. Their spatial structures, seen in the longitudinal section drawings, dovetail and overlap, like a horizontal spinal column following the contour of the terrain.

A large structure marks the crest of the hill. The self-contained apartments each have individual entrances, stairwells, and beautiful views. The bedrooms look out on the beech woods where the sun rises; the living spaces are like verandas, with their broad side along the building façade facing the evening sun and looking toward the Sundgau hills.

Rindermarkt Apartment Building, Zurich
1988

GEWÜRZ HANDLUNG   CHINA   TEE

92

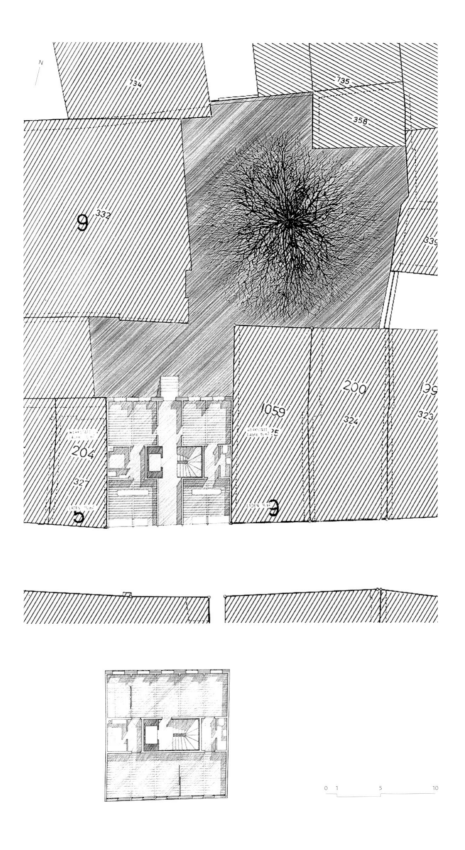

I always enjoy looking over the bid we submitted to this competition in 1988.
I see in it a small piece of Arte Povera, with historical references, simple
constructive logic, gray painted wood, clattering sliding shutters, a roof terrace,
and a so-called *Zinne*, or battlement, as is typical of the Old Town in Zurich.
The façade in the courtyard is overgrown with wild grapevines, the gray painted
wood is meant to look like sandstone, as is the case with many window and
door frames in the simpler buildings of the Old Town. It was also a priority for us
to keep the courtyard in back free. We visualized a great, solitary tree in the
space. It was our intention to create, with sparse means, a dense atmosphere full
of echoes of the familiar and the quotidian.
The façades of the dilapidated building were originally meant to be replaced
by the new construction, but were ultimately preserved.

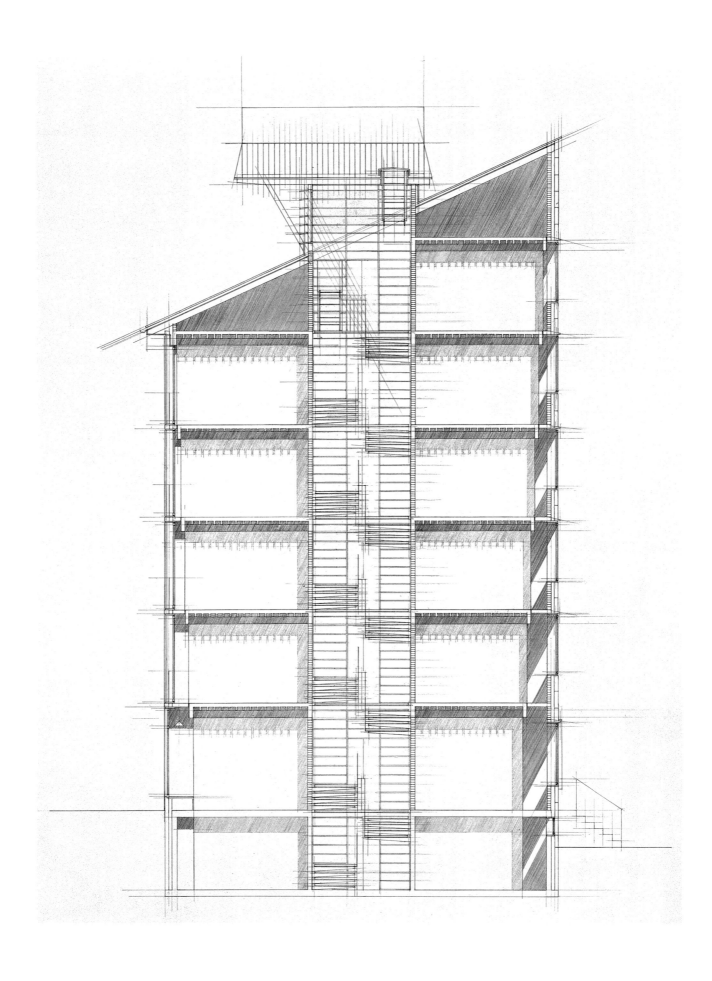

Rothorn Mountaintop Restaurant and Gondola Station,
Valbella, Graubünden
1989–1990

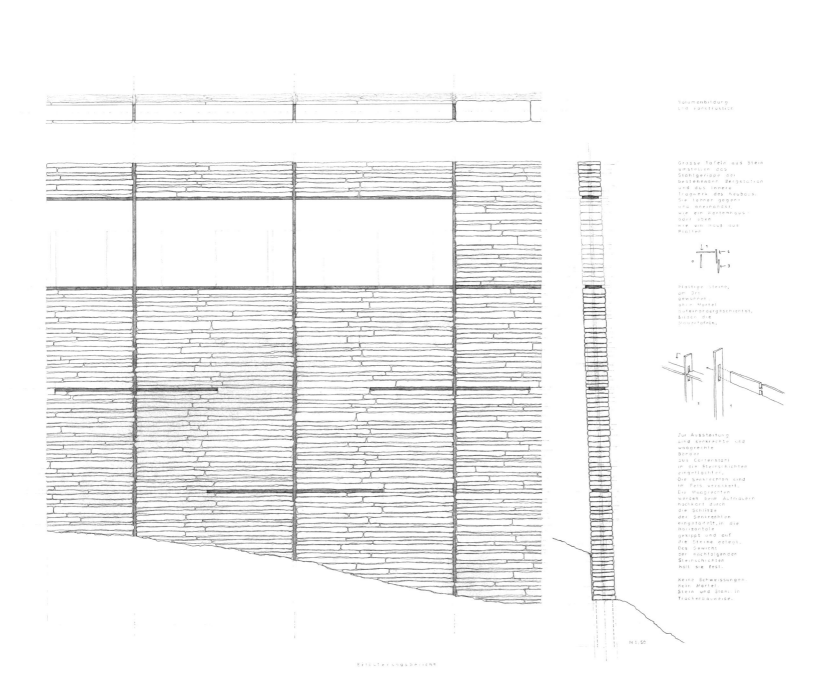

The study for the new gondola station on the Rothorn, a good two thousand meters above sea level, gave us the opportunity to think about a kind of dry-wall masonry, a compound of steel and stone. Our ambition was to bind the rocks of the mountaintop together without using mortar, and to interweave them with steel parts for structural stability.

The ancient tradition of building by piling up local stone in layers has always fascinated me. I have a weakness for buildings that seem to grow out of the landscape. Anyone who is familiar with the old stone houses that were built at this altitude in the Alps will also have a sense of the atmosphere we wanted to conjure inside the building: unheated, open halls with flat, laminar stones carefully stacked up to make walls, and daylight peeking through in certain places; public areas with an inner cladding of massive woodwork made from beams, floorboards, and planks.

When I think back on the drafts we came up with and recall the spatial atmosphere I was dreaming of, I feel I have a stockpile of mental images for the theme of high-altitude construction that I have yet to exhaust. These images deal with powerful structures, elemental constructions, and large-scale dimensions.

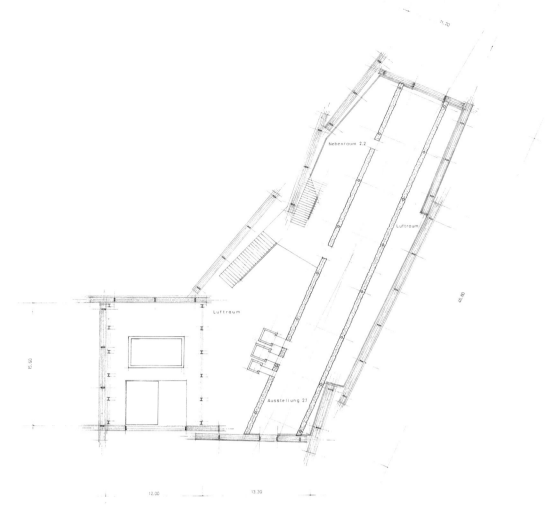

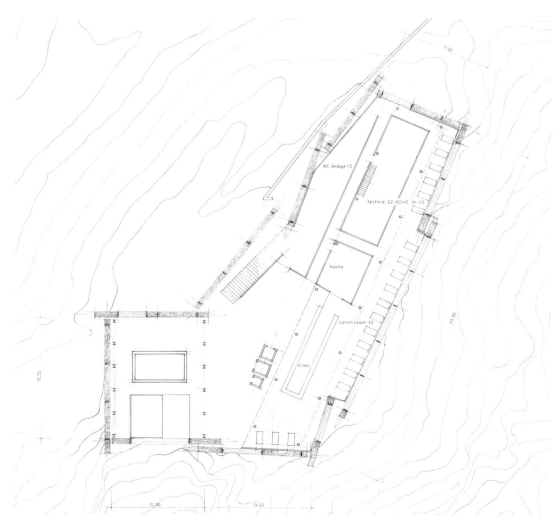

104

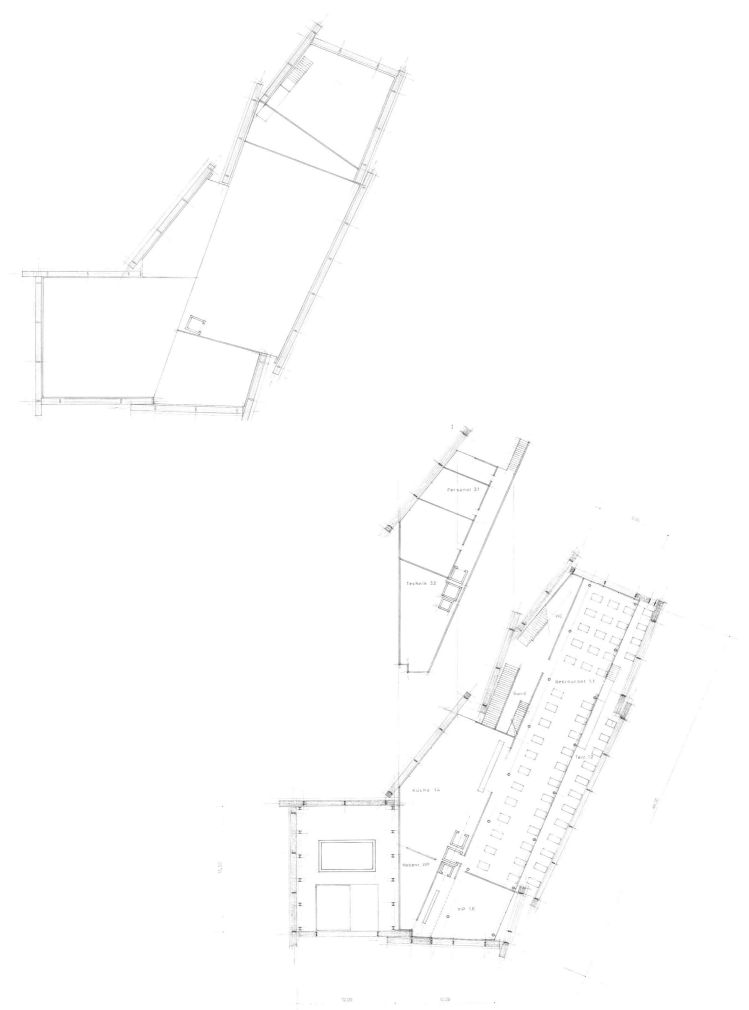

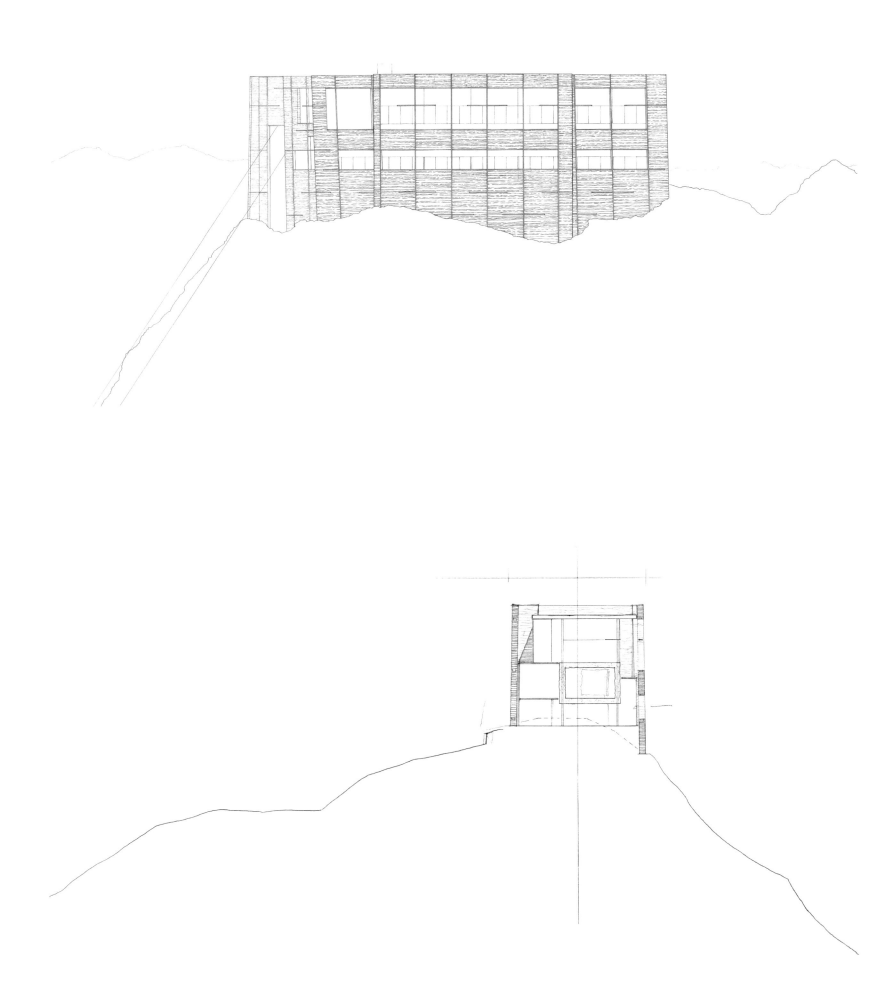

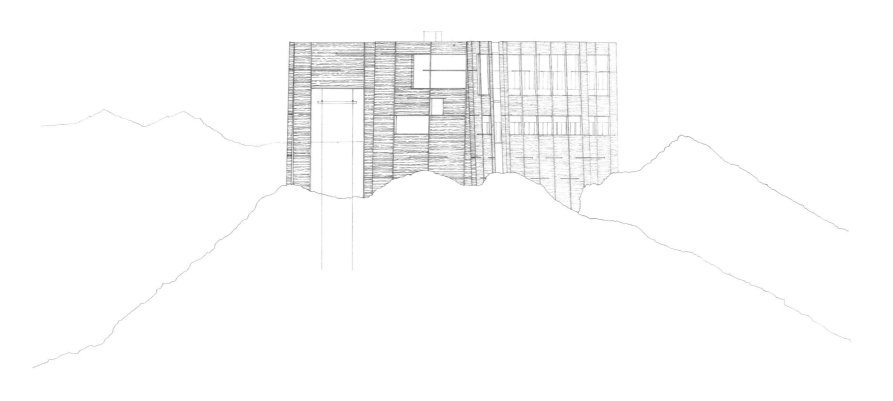

Apartments for Senior Citizens, Masans, Chur, Graubünden

1989 – 1993

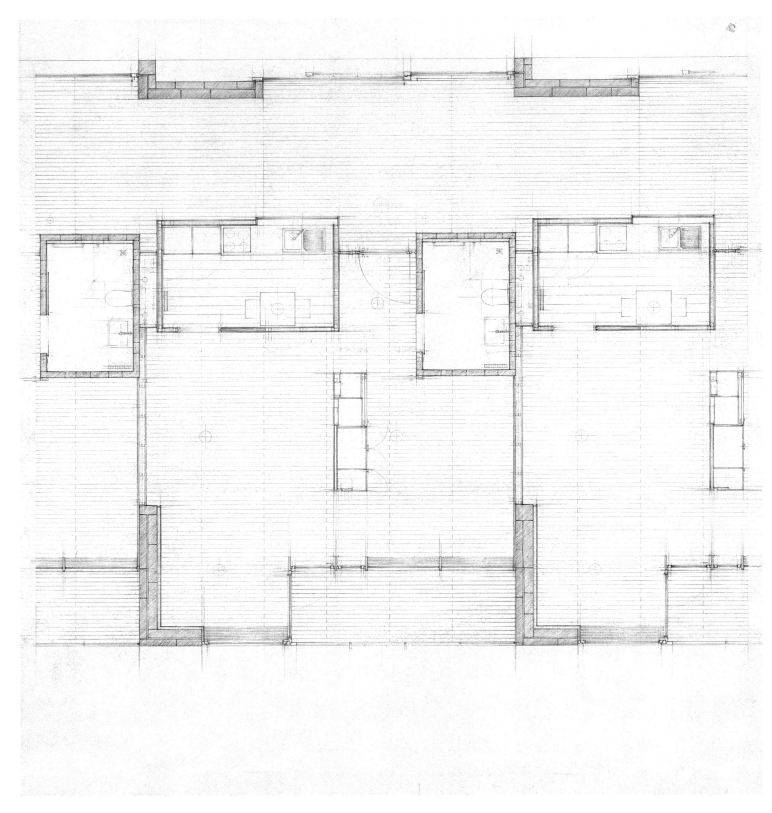

Z —

0   1   2

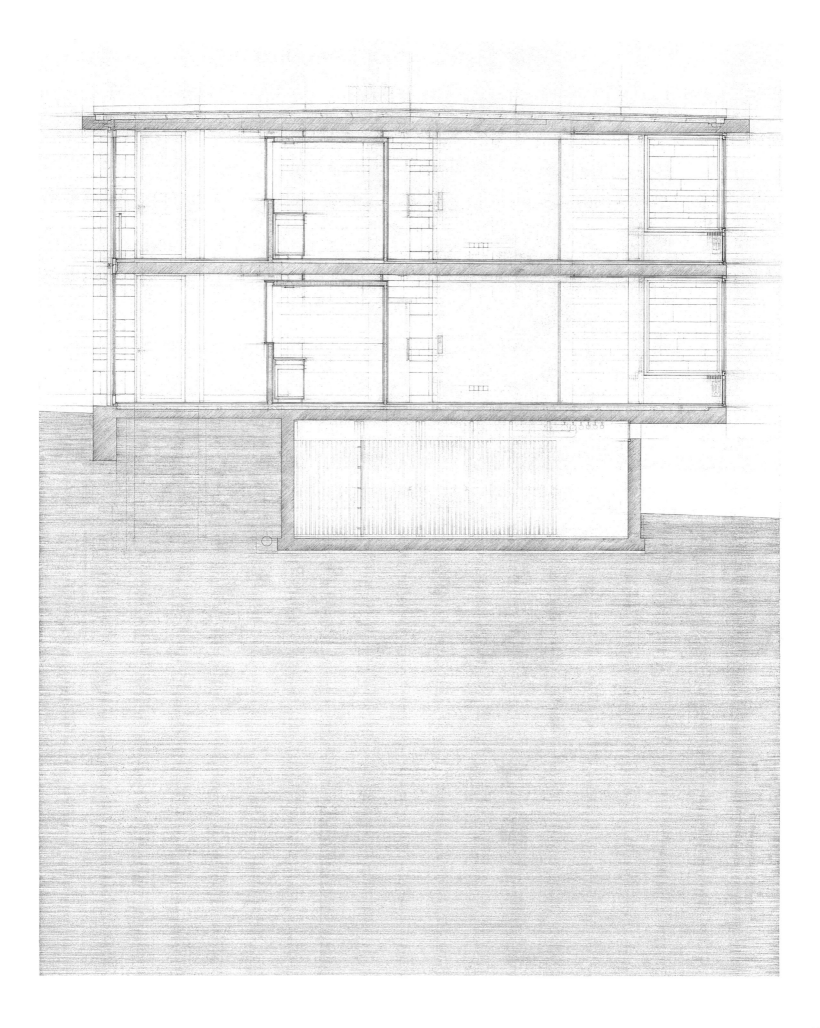

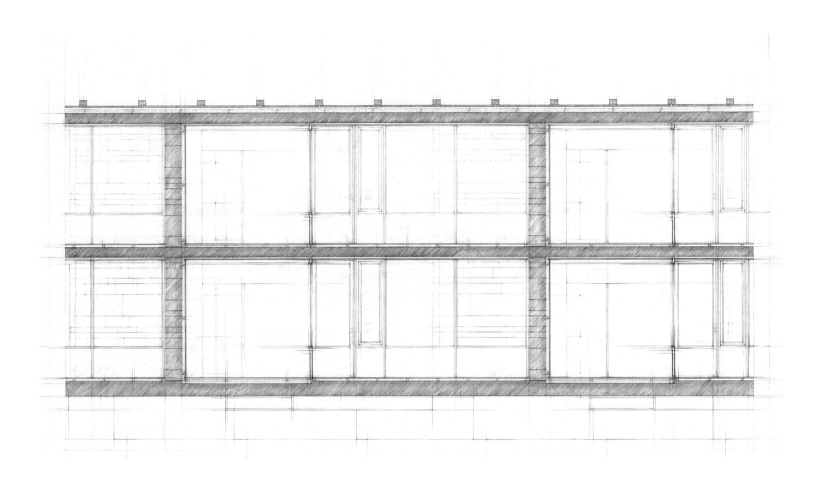

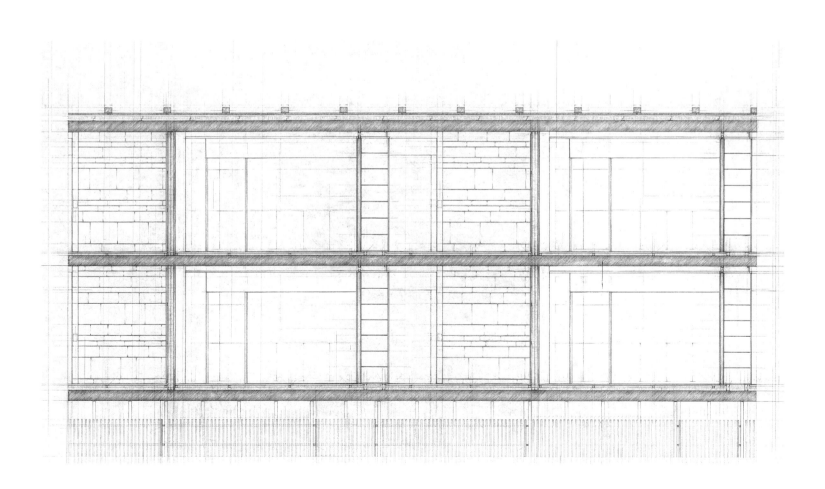

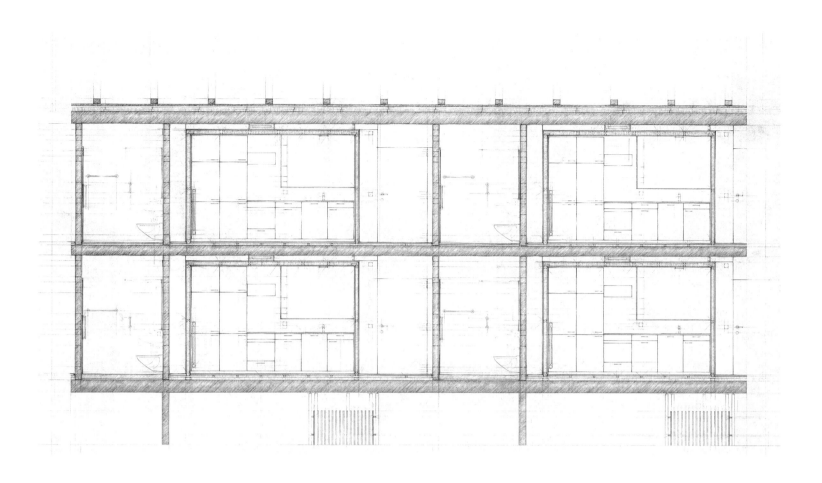

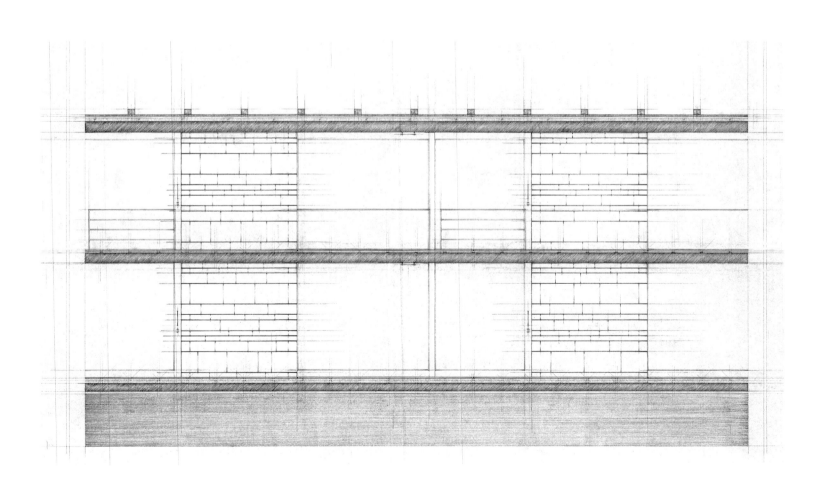

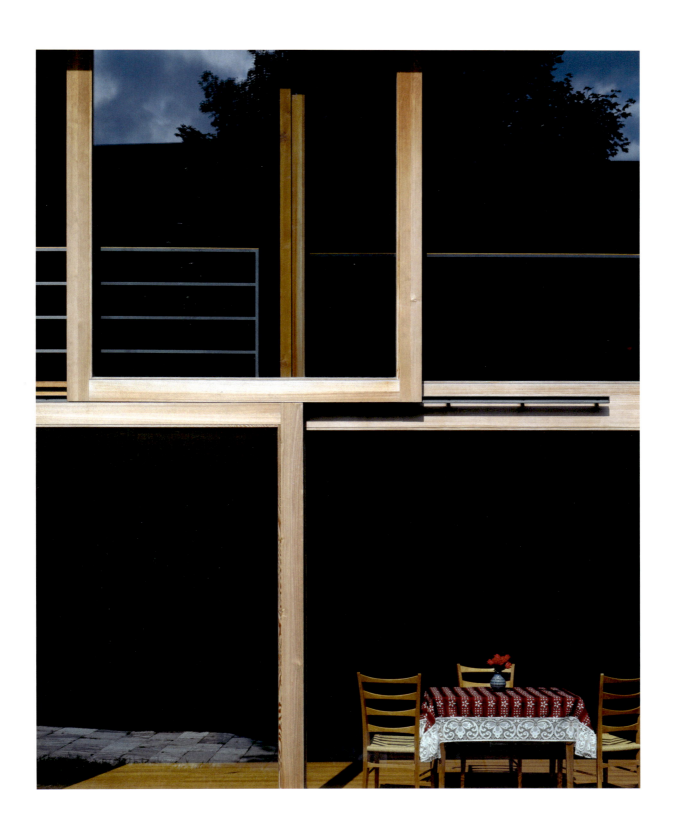

The circumstances must have been favorable, for today I realize that we succeeded in building a rather elegant senior citizens' residence for ordinary people within the framework of the budget granted by the state. We designed the new structure from the inside out. We tried to keep in mind the twilight years of people who have had to leave their homes and apartments in the villages around Chur to live here in an assisted-living environment: the structure is part of a nursing home for the elderly. The number of rooms and the size of the apartments were prescribed by the client; everything else—the architectural feeling, the materials used—came out of the idea of offering something that the occupants knew, liked, and could easily use: a bay window in the living room looks out onto the evening sun, the balconies are placed in niches protected from the wind, the kitchen window opens out to the entrance hall and encourages social contact. This entrance hall is larger than a regular corridor so that the occupants can set up the area outside their apartment with their own furniture and personal articles from their former homes, sit there and have a chat with their neighbors, as they once did in the village on a bench outside the house.

The trio of tufa masonry, exposed concrete ceilings, and larch-wood is familiar to the people of this area; it even has something refined about it, for in Graubünden tufa was once used for important public buildings. The waxed larch-wood floors are made of really thick boards fixed on a lath underlay, and they sound like wood when walked upon.

The apartments are popular. Those who want to live there must apply years ahead.

Bregenz Art Museum, Austria
1989 – 1997

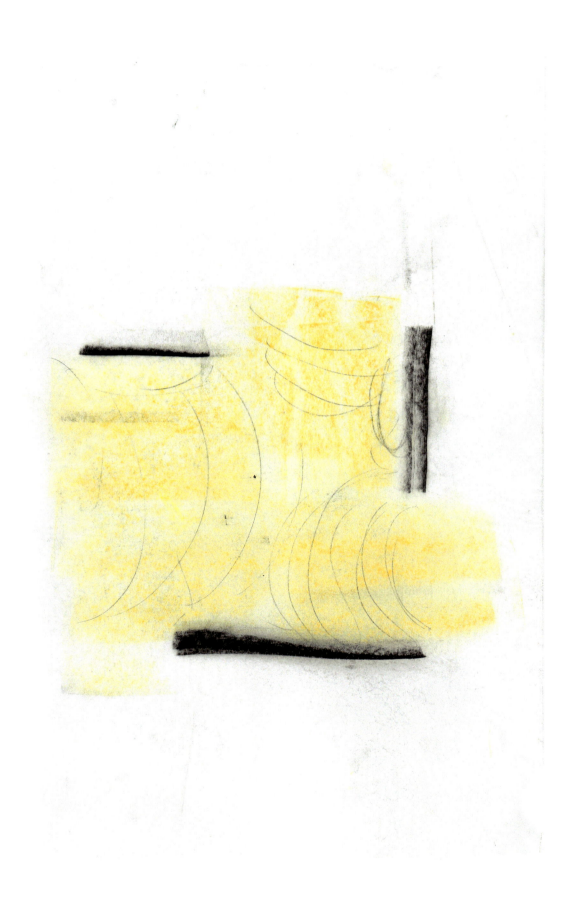

A fine haze floating over the water, a radiance hanging in the air: the light of Lake Constance. Our dream was to capture this light in the spaces of the new art museum in Bregenz. Using the design sketch shown, we worked out how the daylight would enter the exhibition spaces laterally. The three shear walls supporting the stacked spaces would provide shading; different daylight zones would evolve and change with the course of the sun. The daylight entering from the sides gives shape and texture to the spaces; and the viewer senses the orientation, the position of the sun, the time of day. On studying our first 1:10 scale models we had learned it would be possible to have the light from Lake Constance penetrate the building from the side and to conceive the whole structure as a daylight museum. Artificial light can be added as needed, with the daylight dimmed or totally screened out. The technical means for this has been built into the multilayered façade and the hollow spaces of the translucent daylight ceilings.

Daylight hits etched glass. The etching on the glass diffuses the light evenly. The building façade made of large air-flushed glass panels and the similarly constructed glass ceilings of the interior play with this effect. Between these outer and inner glass membranes there is a sealed liner of insulated glass which in the upper stories is hidden by the free-hanging glass panes of the ceilings. This is what gives the impression of light freely entering the exhibition space.

The museum is conceived in terms of its material makeup; it is no "white cube," no abstract white shell, of the kind espoused by many artists as an antidote to the narcissistic architectural productions widespread at the time. Its material presence was important to us: exposed concrete, polished concrete, and steel and glass of various qualities. We thought that works of art would profit from this explicit materiality, deliberately presented with understated, industrial clarity. We wished to have a physical, sensual framework for art.

Studying the new museum site from an urban planning perspective elicited the wish to have a proud new structure arise amid the random array of buildings along the lakeshore. The organizer of the competition, the Austrian state of Vorarlberg, wanted the new museum to function as a beacon for the whole Lake Constance region. We embraced this wish and applied it not just to the exhibits that the building would accommodate, but to the structure itself.

Our decision to organize the museum as four stories rather than build it flat, which would easily have been possible on the available land, had far-reaching consequences.

The shape of the museum is an early and welcome outcome of choosing a cube instead of a one-story layout. I had not thought about this: artists love to have their art animate an entire building. Artists and curators setting up their exhibitions in the museum today enjoy and benefit from the run of four stories stacked on top of one another. Four large spaces, vertically arranged, vividly lit: a tall entrance level with light from the side, two middle stories, also laterally illuminated through glass ceilings, and a slightly taller top floor, its sidelight somewhat more intense at this height; all four spaces built on the same footprint and connected via a circuit of staircases. This arrangement makes for a strong architectural unity. The visitor's experience is informed by the easily comprehensible structure of the museum. The size of the building is also felicitous. The exhibitions can be viewed in a single visit. The architectural framework has an element of domesticity and intimacy.

The concentration of the structural volume around a point on the lake side of the site yielded a further benefit. It allowed us to free up a space on the Old City side of the parcel. We created a little plaza on this spot, which today is called Karl-Tizian-Platz, and we responded to part of the client's specifications by proposing a separate administration building with a restaurant café on the ground floor. Placed as a freestanding structure in front of the museum cube, it relates to the State Theater's arcade passageway and establishes a link to the Old City.

The idea has become reality: visitors drinking their coffee on the square have a view of the museum entrance and can watch the comings and goings on the edge of the Old City. Public space, urban energy.

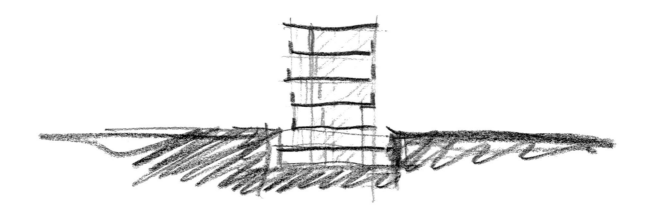

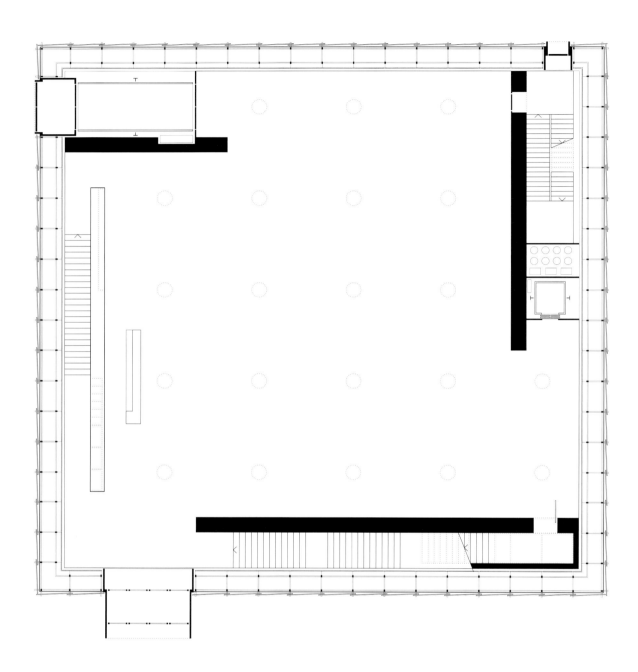

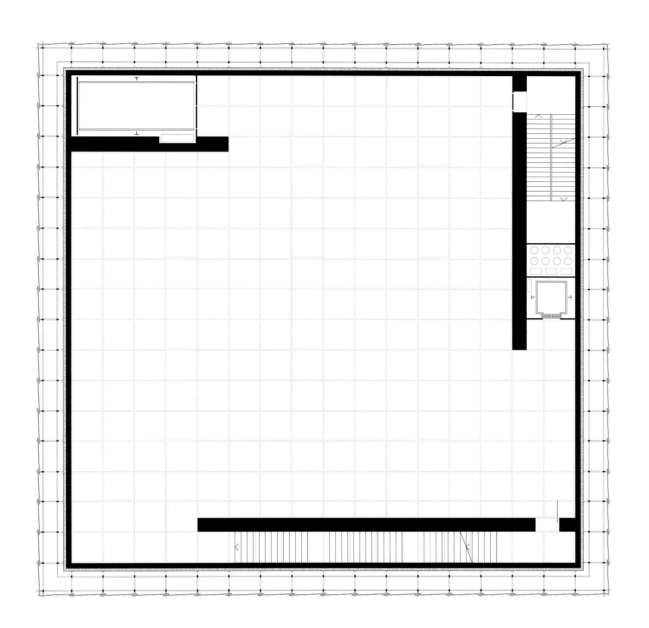

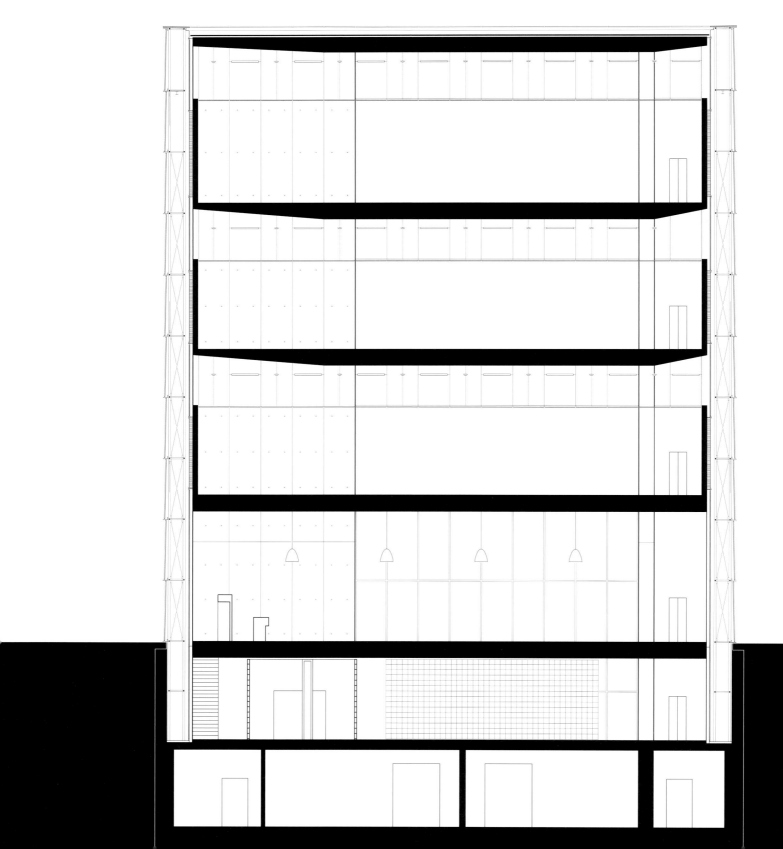

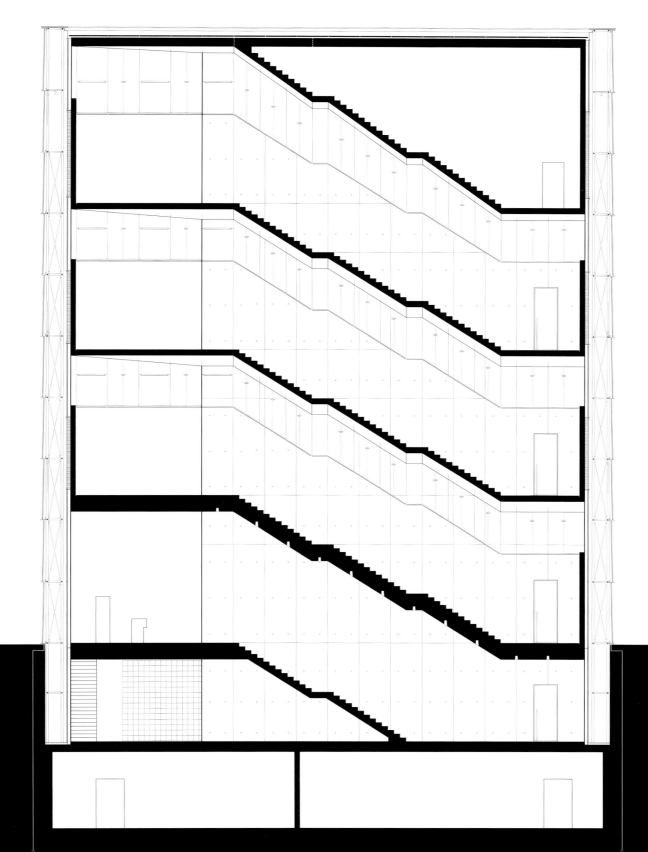

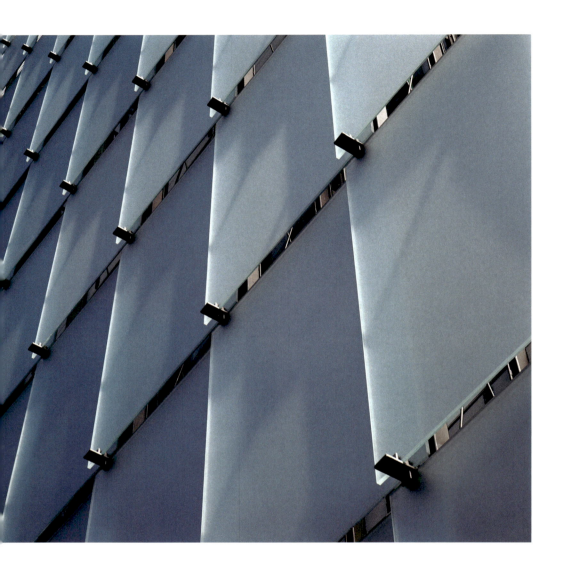

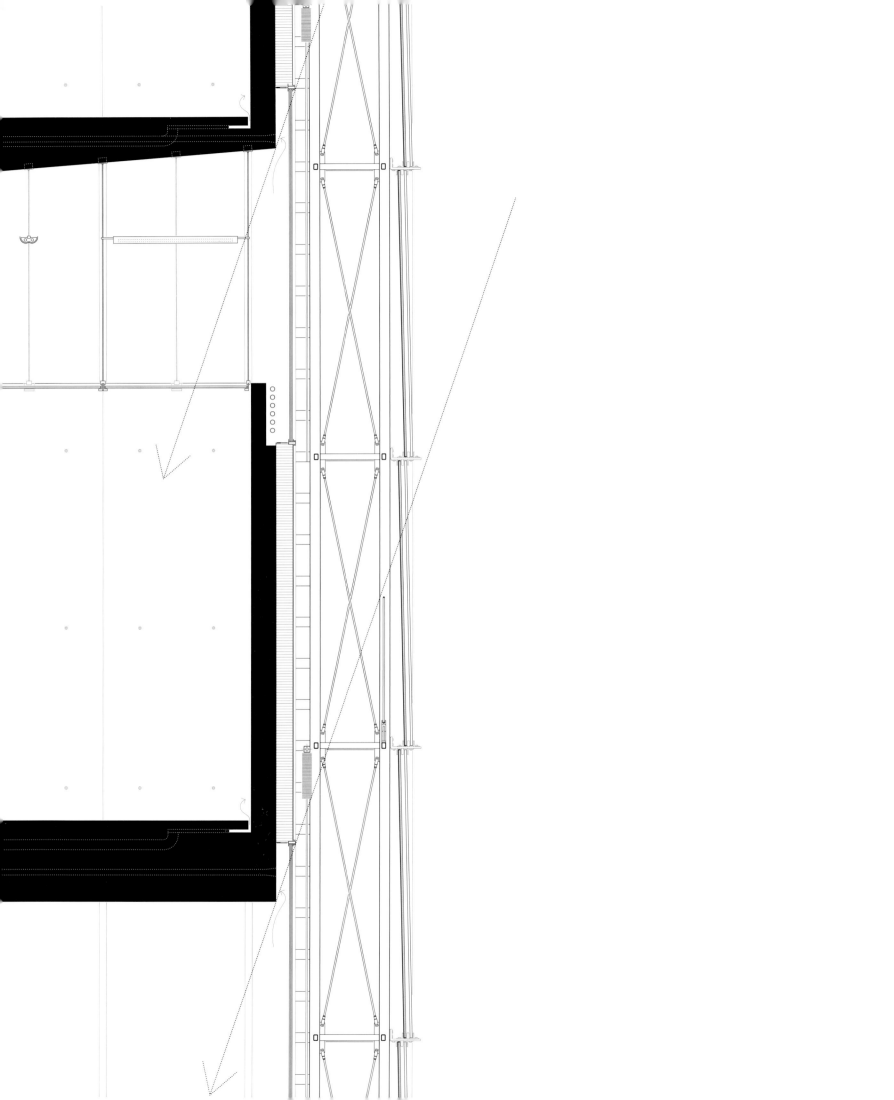

Concept: Peter Zumthor, Thomas Durisch, Beat Keusch
Design: Beat Keusch Visuelle Kommunikation, Basel – Beat Keusch,
Angelina Köpplin
Artistic advice: Arpaïs Du Bois
Translation: John Hargraves
Editing: Catherine Schelbert
Proofreading: Bronwen Saunders
Image processing: Georg Sidler, Samuel Trutmann
Printing and binding: DZA Druckerei zu Altenburg GmbH, Thüringen

Epigraph
Ilse Aichinger, *Kleist, Moos, Fasane*
© S. Fischer Verlag GmbH, Frankfurt am Main, 1987, p. 37

Picture credits, see appendix, volume 5

This book is volume 1 of *Peter Zumthor 1985–2013,* a set of five
volumes which are not available separately.

© 2014 Verlag Scheidegger & Spiess AG, Zurich

New edition 2024: ISBN 978-3-03942-248-7

German edition: ISBN 978-3-03942-247-0

Verlag Scheidegger & Spiess AG
Niederdorfstrasse 54
8001 Zurich
Switzerland

Scheidegger & Spiess is being supported by the Federal Office of
Culture with a general subsidy for the years 2021–2024.

www.scheidegger-spiess.ch